Anita & Ed

Welcome to Louisville.

I hope you enjoy the images in this
book... And if not Recall the

gallery owner's refrain: "As we
could not find the artist,
We hung his picture".

Keith

THE PHOTOGRAPHIC humor OF

For me, reality resides in intuition and imagination,
and in the small voice in my head which says,
'Isn't that extraordinary?!' –Duane Michals

KEITH AUERBACH

ISBN 978-0-9797310-0-6

This book was produced and designed by *New Blue Creative Communications* and *StudioFolio* of Louisville, Kentucky. The cover concept, using Platelet font, came from Keith Kleespies. All photographs are by Keith Auerbach. The tritone cover-image inks are black, PMS 406 and PMS 877, and the interior duotone inks are black and PMS 406. The book was printed by *Impressions Incorporated*, Louisville, Kentucky on 129 pound HannoArt White Gloss Cover and 100 pound HannoArt Silk Text.

The secret to a good sermon is to have a good beginning and a good ending, and to have the two as close together as possible. ~George Burns

(And that's the way I feel about artists' statements.)

I love taking pictures.

I see humor in ordinary instances, and I try to photograph in such a way that the images become intimate comments on living. I photograph feelings and moods and enjoy anticipating, then capturing, the one moment when the picture is perfectly ripe.

I love telling stories.

I have been told there is always a human presence in my photographs whether or not there are people in the image. And I enjoy creating visual puns, unexpected pairings, and a friendly but unfamiliar view of the familiar. Mostly, I watch and wait for that one decisive moment when the ocean can be measured in a drop.

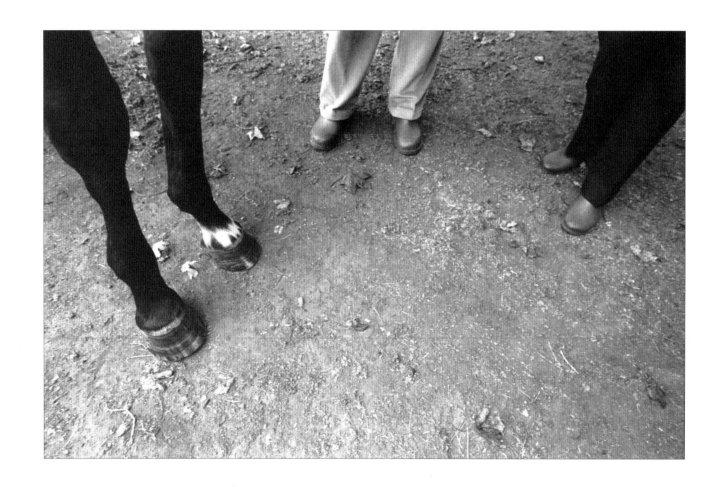

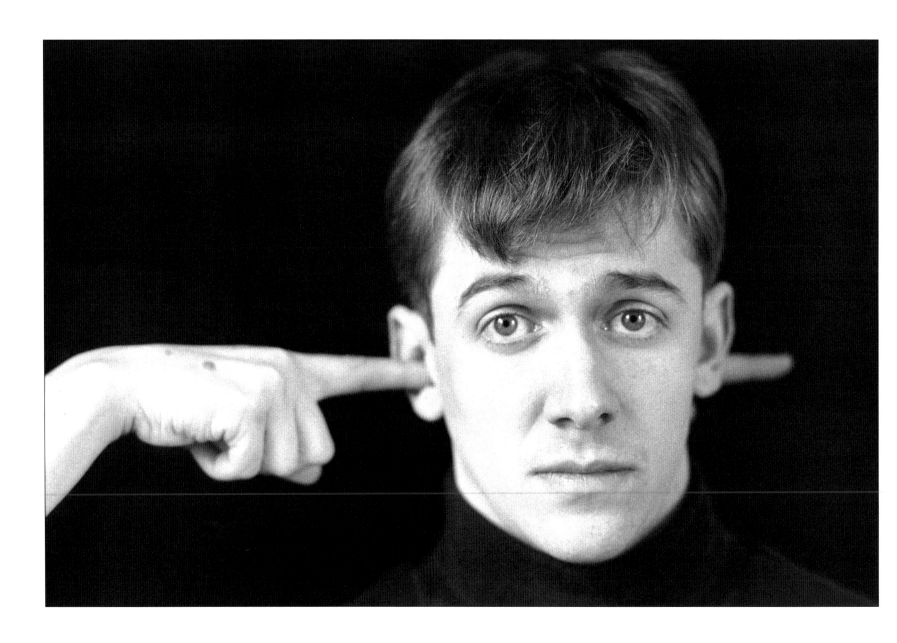

4 **Duckzilla**

5 **Intimate Moment**

6 **Look Back**

7 **The Conversation**

8 **Cuban Car**

9 **The Driver**

10 **Harleigh on Vacation**

11 **Libraire**

12 **Chartres Dog**

13 **Charlie Chaplin**

14 **The Queen and Her Man**

15 **HCFD**

16 **San Francisco Dalmatian**

17 **Disembodied Head at the Louvre**

18 **MARTA and the Mortician**

19 **Alex Confounded**

20 **Two Horses/Six Moons**

21 **Three Eiffel Towers**

22 **En Beaute**

23–24 **Emergence**

25 **Crib Hand**

26 **Moments Before the Pounce**

28 **The Leaver and the Left**

29 **Boots and Paws**

30 **Yoga Man and His Dog**

31 **Derby Day Infield Convicts**

32 **English Binoculars**

33 **The Kiss**

34 **After the Kiss**

35 **Putt-Putt**

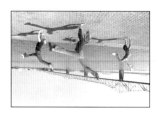

36 **River Runners**

37 **Sand Shark Castle**

38 **Sandy at the Beach**

39 **Bird Brains**

40 **Micro Heads at the Met**

41 **Perigieux, France**

42 **French Man and His Dog**

43 **Hatter and His Harem**

44 **Cow Convention**

45 **Les Halles Sculpture**

46 **The Eye**

47 **Hot Tongues**

48 **Shirt Face**

49 **The Divers**

50 **Three Horses/Two Riders**

51 **The Tumblers**

52 **Water Cannon Mouth**

53–54 **Angel**

55 **Elongated Star**

56 **The Falling Diver**

57 **Hot Caution**

58 **Leading the Dead**

59 **Donkey Love**

60 **The Eiffel Kiss**

61 **Painting Legs**

62 **Pair of Clasped Hands**

63 **Maillol and Lovers**

64 **Zurich Monster with Elderly Twins**

65 **Three Stages of Romance**

66 **Italian Headrest**

67 **Marccain Mannequins**

68 **Bourdeilles Cow**

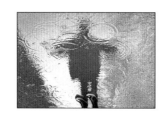

69 **Rain Shadow**

70 **Luci**

72 **London Looks**

73 **Finger Head**

74 **A Man Faced Dog**

75 **Shareef Dancer**

76 **Cow Lick**

77 **Hunt Dog Nose**

78 **Naples Bird**

80 **Centaur**

81–82 **Snow Trees**

Photographic Exhibitions, Awards and Publications

2007
PYRO Gallery
Louisville, KY
Solo Show
*The Photographic Humor
of Keith Auerbach*

SoHo Photo Gallery
New York, NY
National Competition Exhibition
Mia Fineman, juror
SoHo Photo Competition

Center for Women and Families
Louisville, KY
Group Show

2006
PYRO Gallery
Group Show
*All It Takes for Evil to Prevail …
Art and Social Justice*

Jewish Community Center
Louisville, KY
PYRO Photographers

Glassworks
Louisville, KY
Two Person Show
Hot Dogs – Art About Canines

Glassworks
Group Show

2005
PYRO Gallery
Solo Show
Horse Sense and Sensibility

Gallery at Actors Theatre
Louisville, KY
Humana Festival of
New American Plays
Three Person Show
What is Photography?

PYRO Gallery
*Emergence: A Group Exhibition
for Spring*

2004
Gallery at Actors Theatre
Group Show
Selected Works from PYRO Artists

PYRO Gallery
Group Show
Female Nude Exhibition

2003
PYRO Gallery
Group Show
New Work

2001
Louisville Science Center
Louisville, KY
15 prints in permanent exhibition
The World Within Us

1999
Physicians Art Museum
Louisville, KY
13 prints in permanent art collection

1997
Artswatch
Louisville, KY
Group Exhibition

Metro Louisville Journalism Awards
Photography – Magazine and Feature

1996
Metro Louisville Journalism Awards
Photography – Magazine and Feature

1995
Bank One Gallery
Louisville, KY
Good Dog

1990–94
Kentucky State Fair – 29 Ribbons
1993 Best of Show

1994
Louisville Visual Art Association
International Group Exhibition
Mainz, Germany
Works on Paper

Metro United Way
Louisville, KY
Group Exhibition
Images of Strength and Service

1993
Louisville Visual Art Association
Group Exhibition
Works on Paper

The Photo Review
Published Juried Show
Duane Michals, juror

1992
The Center for Photography
at Woodstock
Woodstock, NY
Published Juried Show
Larry Link, juror
The Family of Man – Revisited

National Dog Show
Wichita, KS
Art Show at the Dog Show
1 Ribbon

American Photo Magazine
Published Juried Show
Annual Photo Contest Issue

1991
Gallery at Actors Theatre
Solo Show
Familiar Fictions

1990
The Courier-Journal Photo Contest
2 Awards

1971
Chicago, IL
Group Exhibition
Columbia, MD
One Man Show

1970
Northwestern University
Evanston, IL
Group Show
Photography Contest Winner

Chicago Magazine
Published Juried Show

acknowledgements

I want to give special thanks for encouragement and inspiration to Jean Henderson, Suzanne Mitchell, CJ Pessma and Duane Michals for their kindness and thoughtful words. Thanks to Sheila Metzner, Joyce Tenneson, John Paul Caponigro and Maggie Taylor who have also contributed to my evolution as an artist.

And my appreciation goes to Suzi Zimmerer, Keith Kleespies, Meg Higgins, Bob Hower and CJ Pressma for their persistent support and good humor in producing this book.

Each artist seems to be the native of an unknown country. *~Proust*